GLORIOUS BUTTERFLIES
and their flora

EIGHT PAINTINGS OF THE BRITISH BUTTERFLIES
WITH THEIR NECTAR AND CATERPILLAR FOODPLANTS

BY

VALERIE BAINES F.L.S

EDITED BY

David Dunbar

WITH CONTRIBUTIONS BY:

DAVID DUNBAR
JOHN FELTWELL
ROBERT GOODDEN
GAIL JEFFCOATE
PETER NEWTON-LEWIS
ANDREW PHILLIPS
ALAN STUBBS
MARGARET VICKERY
KEN WILLMOTT

**BUTTERFLY
CONSERVATION**

PUBLISHED BY BUTTERFLY CONSERVATION

Published by Butterfly Conservation
The British Butterfly Conservation Society Ltd.
P.O. Box 222, Dedham, Nr. Colchester, Essex CO7 6EY
Telephone: (0206) 322342

Design and Typesetting by
Quetzal Publications
6 Corinthian Close, Basingstoke,
Hampshire RG22 4TN
Telephone: (0256) 478309

ISBN 0 9512452 8 7

All profits from the sales proceeds of this book go to Butterfly Conservation, a charity, which is dedicated to saving wild butterflies and their habitats.

CONTENTS

INTRODUCTION

BY VALERIE BAINES

Butterfly Conservation asked me to paint the British butterflies to mark the 25th Anniversary of the Society's foundation. Knowing that it is now taking a leading role in conservation and is the world's largest entomological society, I was honoured and delighted to accept the commission.

The prospect of portraying nearly seventy different species of butterflies, not to mention their caterpillar foodplants was a daunting challenge, but at the same time here was a wonderful opportunity. I have always loved butterflies and have admired the work of artists both past and present who have drawn and painted these 'living jewels'.

In the 18th Century the exquisite work of Moses Harris is recorded by the superb hand-coloured engravings in his book *The Aurelian*. The accuracy and detail of the engravings after H. N. Humphreys in his *British Butterflies and their Transformations* published in 1841 was a further milestone in butterfly art. F. W. Frohawk was the first to depict fully the life-cycles of all the British butterflies in his magnificent *Natural History* nearly 70 years ago. His illustrations are probably unsurpassed for reference purposes and display his extraordinary skill both as an artist and as an observer of nature.

My task was, therefore, to find a new approach to the subject matter which had already been exhaustively covered by so many great artists. In fact, this did not turn out to be as difficult as one might have imagined. The very reasons for the existence of Butterfly Conservation were just the inspiration I needed. First of all, the amazing variety and beauty of butterflies is a gift from nature of which everyone should be aware. They have a great value to the environment although they are not safe and their survival is under threat. Conservation and the plants needed by butterflies for survival was therefore the underlying theme that I adopted.

The choice of butterflies under the heading of each painting has, in some instances, been somewhat arbitrary. Our commoner butterflies are shown in the first four pictures under a likely, but not exclusive, habitat of each one by using the headings of 'Garden', 'Countryside', 'Grassland' and 'Woodland'. The other four headings relate to the status of those butterflies which are localised, live in specialised habitats, or are under serious threat. Finally, there are the migrants and those butterflies which are extinct. In the last section Andrew Phillips of Butterfly Conservation describes how Butterfly Conservation is helping to save butterflies.

As botany is another of my great loves, I have enjoyed composing my paintings with the caterpillar foodplants and some butterfly nectar flowers as well - flowers and butterflies giving life to each other.

Both Butterfly Conservation and I are extremely grateful to the authors of the highly informative and entertaining commentaries which accompany each picture - our thanks go to them all.

During the year spent on this project I have been fortunate enough to enjoy the generous assistance of many kind people. In particular I should like to thank David Dunbar, Brian Norman, Ron and Christine Foord, Gina Douglas of the Linnean Society, Dr. Bernard Watts, Rob Still, Nigel Spring, Gillian Peachey, John Keylock, David Chubb and Rosemary Titterington.

In the past it was fashionable to make collections of butterflies by catching and pinning them out in cabinets. Such collecting is, in a way understandable, as an attempt to perpetuate their beauty and fascination. Today we understand better the need to conserve living butterflies so that they can be enjoyed in their natural surroundings. I hope very much that my paintings have captured at least some of the colour and life of *"Glorious Butterflies"*.

Valerie Baines
January 1993

The Plates

Butterflies in the Garden

BY DR. MARGARET VICKERY

Butterflies dancing in a sunlit garden! An idyllic picture, but one that may be seen on any warm, sunny day in late summer in gardens such as this. Sheltered and full of the cottage garden plants loved by butterflies, it cannot fail to attract these beautiful insects. No scentless roses, regimented flower beds or closely-mown turf here.

Bright Nasturtiums not only produce nectar but their round, green leaves are food for the caterpillars of the Large White and Small White butterflies (you can see one nibbling away). Planted in the vegetable garden Nasturtiums will help to keep the 'cabbage whites' away from the cabbages!

Our garden is not a tidy one, there are Stinging Nettles and flowering grasses to be seen. A swathe of fine grass such as the Annual Meadow-grass shown in the picture tempts the Meadow Brown to pause and lay her eggs. Although not as colourful as other garden visitors the Meadow Brown has a beauty all her own and depicts the very essence of summer. It is one of our most plentiful and commonly-found species throughout the country.

The caterpillars of the Peacock, Small Tortoiseshell, Comma and Red Admiral all use Stinging Nettles as their foodplants. It is not easy to persuade butterflies to lay their eggs on nettles in gardens, generally because these weeds are relegated to a dark corner where the soil is too poor to grow anything else. Our butterflies look for a large patch of healthy plants with nutritious green leaves growing in a sheltered, sunny position in soil fed with compost or manure.

There is one more foodplant in the picture. Ivy flower buds are eaten by Holly Blue caterpillars in summer (the spring brood eats Holly buds). Holly Blues are just as successful at breeding in gardens as the cabbage whites, but their activities are less upsetting to gardeners! The loss of a few Holly or Ivy berries is a small price to pay for the joy of seeing this snippet of sky blue dashing across the garden or patrolling ivy-clad walls and fences.

Our garden is a hive of activity. The Small White is drinking from a water drop on a Nasturtium leaf. The Large White female is resting, probably after laying a batch of eggs. The male Meadow Brown is resting on a grass stem, while the female is feeding from the copious nectar produced by the many flowerlets of the Ice Plant. The Red Admiral has been feasting there for some time. An exotic butterfly this, maybe a visitor from Europe, wafted over on a southerly breeze.

The female Holly Blue, with her black-edged wings, is searching the ivy for a suitable place to lay her eggs, while the male takes a well-earned rest on a leaf before continuing his flight.

The Comma feeding on the Buddleia has its wings closed and is clearly showing the white comma mark on the underwing. The ragged wings of the flying Comma show that it is a male, probably patrolling his territory ready to repel any other butterfly that might enter his air space.

Also feeding on Buddleia, the best nectar plant by far, the two Small Tortoiseshells and the Peacock are oblivious to their surroundings. Their only object in life at this time of the year is to drink as much nectar as possible before finding a safe hibernation place to sleep the winter away. Hopefully, they will survive the many dangers and emerge to fill the spring garden with their beauty and start nature's wonderful cycle all over again.

Butterflies in the Garden

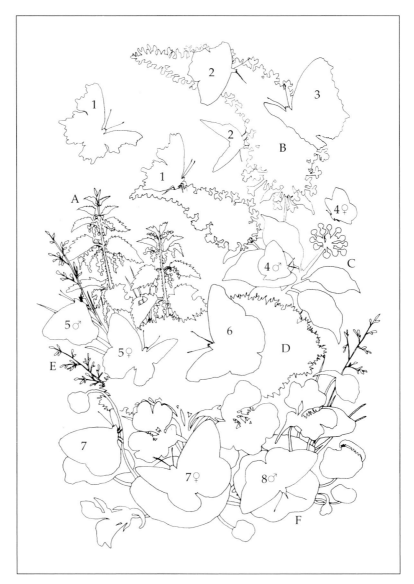

BUTTERFLIES IN THE GARDEN

1	Comma	*Polygonia c-album*
2	Small Tortoiseshell	*Aglais urticae*
3	Peacock	*Inachis io*
4	Holly Blue	*Celastrina argiolus*
5	Meadow Brown	*Maniola jurtina*
6	Red Admiral	*Vanessa atalanta*
7	Large White	*Pieris brassicae*
8	Small White	*Pieris rapae*

A	Stinging Nettle	*Urtica dioica*
B	Buddleia	*Buddleia davidii*
C	Ivy	*Hedera helix*
D	Sedum	*Sedum spectabile*
E	Annual Meadow-grass	*Poa annua*
F	Nasturtium	*Tropaeolum majus*

Countryside Butterflies

BY DAVID DUNBAR

This beautiful painting depicts some of the common species found in our countryside - the natural home of butterflies. Watching butterflies should be unhurried - "Linger and look" was good advice from the late L. Hugh Newman, a well-known butterfly enthusiast and writer. On a warm summer's day stroll across meadows or along the hedgerow and you will always be rewarded by the sight of butterflies.

Larger, brightly-coloured butterflies are conspicuous. However, others are less easily observed or identified because of their small size, quick flight and perhaps camouflage. Whether exploring new territory, busily feeding on nectar flowers or basking in the sun, these are the familiar butterflies you may see almost anywhere.

A mild spring day will awaken the Brimstone out of hibernation. It is one of the longest-lived butterflies, often surviving for up to eleven months. During winter it finds protection amongst the leaves of Holly or Ivy. Early writers suggest that the Brimstone is the "butter-coloured fly" from which the word "butterfly" derives.

Another familiar butterfly at this time of the year is the Orange Tip - only the male displays the distinctive orange forewing markings whilst the white female may often be mistaken for a "cabbage white". She lays her eggs singly on the flower heads of Lady's Smock. The solitary caterpillars, being cannibalistic, may eat a rival encountered on the same plant!

At a glance the Green-veined White is hard to distinguish from the other whites - only when resting can the blackish veins on the upper wings be clearly seen. On the undersides these are broader but fainter and appear green. Inexplicably the vein markings are less pronounced on butterflies emerging later in the season.

By June other familiar butterflies will be appearing. The Wall butterfly is so named for its habit of flying back and forth along the sunny side of a brick wall or fence. In fact, this butterfly is just as frequent on open hillsides where it settles on a stone or bare earth to bask in the sun. If disturbed the butterfly will fly off suddenly but invariably returns to the same resting place a few minutes later. Like the Green-veined White the Wall is double-brooded with a second generation in August.

As with many of the "Blues" it is only the male Common Blue which flaunts brilliant blue wing colouration, whereas the female is a dowdy brown. Both sexes have an intricate underside pattern of pretty orange and black spots on a grey background.

The Large and Small Skippers are grassland butterflies. Their vibrating wing movements in flight are incredibly fast. When settled the wings are folded back along their thick bodies giving a somewhat moth-like appearance.

The Ringlet, so named because of the cream circles on the hindwing, may inadvertently be mistaken for the Meadow Brown. However, the Ringlet is less widespread, possibly because of its preference for damp, grassy habitats. For a short while after its emergence from the chrysalis the wings have an almost velvet texture with a narrow white margin round the edges. Soon they become torn and drab as the butterfly flits amongst the grasses and the white disappears altogether.

The Small Heath may occur on almost any rough grassland and even on mountains up to 2,000 feet. Although rarely seen in large numbers it is one of the most widely distributed butterflies in the British Isles.

And lastly, the delightful Small Copper is often missed because of its quick darting flight. When it feeds on Ragwort or one of its other favourite flowers the glinting coppery red of the wing markings is fully displayed. Like other familiar butterflies the Small Copper has suffered from loss of habitats due to intensive farming methods across the country.

Countryside Butterflies

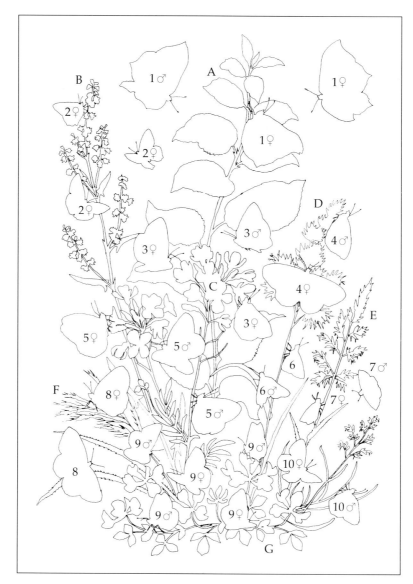

FAMILIAR BUTTERFLIES

1	Brimstone	*Gonepteryx rhamni*
2	Small Copper	*Lycaena phlaeas*
3	Green-veined White	*Pieris napi*
4	Wall	*Lasiommata megera*
5	Orange Tip	*Anthocharis cardamines*
6	Large Skipper	*Ochlodes venata*
7	Small Skipper	*Thymelicus silvestris*
8	Ringlet	*Aphantopus hyperantus*
9	Common Blue	*Polyommatus icarus*
10	Small Heath	*Coenonympha pamphilus*
A	Buckthorn	*Rhamnus catharticus*
B	Sheep's Sorrel (in flower)	*Rumex acetosella*
C	Lady's Smock	*Cardamine pratensis*
D	Cock's-foot	*Dactylis glomerata*
E	Yorkshire Fog	*Holcus lanatus*
F	Wood False-Brome	*Brachypodium sylvaticum*
G	Birdsfoot Trefoil	*Lotus corniculatus*

Grassland Butterflies

BY GAIL JEFFCOATE

In the past, meadows, pastures, verges and hillsides supported a great variety of grasses and wild flowers which provided food for caterpillars and nectar for adult butterflies. Nowadays most grassland has been 'improved' for agriculture and contains only rye grass (not a foodplant for any butterfly) and a few other plants such as thistles and docks. Grassland butterflies have become much scarcer as a result. Fragments of unspoiled grassland remain on steep slopes or other land inhospitable to agriculture such as heathland, and may contain colonies of the butterflies pictured here.

Grassland should be managed by grazing or cutting to prevent coarse vegetation and scrub from taking over. The best habitats for butterflies are sheltered, sunny sites containing a mosaic of tall and short grass and a range of food and nectar plants with shrubs to provide shelter and perching and roosting spots.

The Marbled White is not a member of the white family. It is more closely related to the Meadow Brown and Ringlet, and like them it uses grasses as larval foodplants, especially Red Fescue. The attractive adults fly in July, and are irresistible to photographers when they settle on knapweed or scabious.

Essex Skippers are very similar to Small Skippers but can be distinguished by the black undersides of the antennae tips. They are not confined to Essex, and can be found over a large part of south and east England. Females lay eggs on coarser grasses such as Cock's-foot; the caterpillars protect themselves by spinning leaf edges together to form tunnels.

The wings of the Grayling are used for camouflage and temperature regulation as well as flight. This butterfly prefers a dry, sandy or rocky habitat with sparse vegetation, and most colonies are found on heathland or coastal grass. In August the Chalkhill Blue may be seen flying among Adonis and Common Blues on the southern chalk downs. It is paler blue than its relatives, and shares with the Adonis Blue its dependence on Horseshoe Vetch as a larval foodplant.

Green Hairstreaks live in a variety of habitats and feed on a number of foodplants. The male is territorial and perches on a shrub, darting out to chase off other males or pursue potential mates. The female looks very similar, but is a more retiring insect.

The Rockrose is a foodplant of the Green Hairstreak on chalky grassland, and it is also used by the Brown Argus which occurs mainly in this habitat. The latter has two broods a year, in May-June and August-September.

The Large Heath is a northern species found in damp grassland on bogs and moors. The adult takes nectar from Cross-leaved Heath, while eggs are laid in July and August on Harestail and White Beak-sedge.

Resembling a small, brown moth, the Dingy Skipper is aptly named. The numbers of colonies of this little butterfly have declined as grassland has been destroyed or ploughed and now it mainly inhabits downs, quarries and sheltered coastal grassland. Another moth-like butterfly, the Grizzled Skipper, can also be seen on some downland sites in May. It also breeds in woodland glades where its foodplants, which include Wild Strawberry, Agrimony and Tormentil, grow.

The best way to distinguish the Dark Green Fritillary from other large fritillaries is to examine the underside, but this is not easy as it is a powerful flyer and hard to approach. Now the most widespread of our fritillaries, it feeds on violet plants on coastal grassland, downland, and woodland rides.

Grassland Butterflies

GRASSLAND BUTTERFLIES

1	Marbled White	*Melanargia galathea*
2	Essex Skipper	*Thymelicus lineola*
3	Grayling	*Hipparchia semele*
4	Chalkhill Blue	*Lysandra coridon*
5	Green Hairstreak	*Callophrys rubi*
6	Brown Argus	*Aricia agestis*
7	Large Heath	*Coenonympha tullia*
8	Dingy Skipper	*Erynnis tages*
9	Grizzled Skipper	*Pyrgus malvae*
10	Dark Green Fritillary	*Argynnis aglaja*
A	Red Fescue	*Festuca rubra*
B	Cock's-foot	*Dactylis glomerata*
C	Sheep's Fescue	*Festuca ovina*
D	Horseshoe Vetch	*Hippocrepis comosa*
E	Rockrose	*Helianthemum nummularium*
F	White Beak-Sedge	*Rhyncospora alba*
G	Wild Strawberry	*Fragaria vesca*
H	Marsh Violet	*Viola palustris*

Butterflies in Woodland

BY K. J. WILLMOTT

Open deciduous woodland, especially oak, is by far the most appreciated by British butterflies. Here, wildflowers such as the Bugle in the Spring, Bramble in the Summer and Hemp Agrimony in the Autumn can attract hordes of butterflies on a sunny day.

The cold regimental stands of conifers are shunned by butterflies and many other forms of life. Neglected woodland is similarly poor for butterflies. Most species-rich woodland is in fact regularly maintained. Either the timber is utilised by man or otherwise it is in the hands of conservation organisations and being managed appropriately for wildlife.

The re-establishment of coppice cycles to increase the ground flora such as the important common Dog Violet, widening of shady rides to allow better sunlight penetration, therefore increasing nectar-bearing plants and larval foodplants and the creation of sunny roadside bays are all measures that can benefit the butterfly population of a woodland.

The White-letter Hairstreak feeds exclusively on elm, the larvae feeding upon the leaves of either the Wych or English Elm, wherever they are to be found in the vicinity of woodland. Populations crashed in the early 1970s with the serious outbreak of Dutch Elm disease, but are now recovering.

Oak is the only larval foodplant of the Purple Hairstreak. The females deposit their eggs in July and August on next year's dormant buds. As well as the Sessile and Pedunculate Oaks they will also deposit eggs on the Turkey Oak and possibly other species. The Speckled Wood is perhaps our only species tolerant of shady woodland, but even in this environment males establish transitory territories in shafts of sunlight filtering through the canopy.

One butterfly that seems to signify high summer is the Gatekeeper which normally emerges from the first week of July onwards. The male (pictured) has a dark band of specialised scent scales in the central portion of its forewing. Females are entirely orange, except for the brown borders, and lay their eggs on fine woodland grasses.

The abandonment of coppicing, which increased the number of shady woods, was to the advantage of the White Admiral. This butterfly's graceful flight is a delight to watch as it glides and soars along the woodland tracks. Its larval foodplant, the Honeysuckle, also survived the extra shade and where dappled sunlight bathes a percentage of its leaves, the females are tempted to deposit their sea-urchin like eggs on the edge of a leaf.

Our largest Fritillary, the Silver-washed, requires both open and sunny flower-rich woodland areas and the shade created by tall mature oaks. After locating a supply of Dog Violets on the woodland floor, females flutter up to land on the nearest tree trunk and fly upwards in stages depositing an egg at each stop.

The Small Pearl-bordered Fritillary flies a little later than the Pearl-bordered Fritillary and can be recognised best by the black lines and spots on the under-surface of the wings. The Small Pearl-bordered is also less tolerant of dry, open and hot conditions which are much preferred by the latter species.

Finally, our most superb butterfly, the Purple Emperor, is one that is rarely seen by the casual observer. It spends much of its time high in the canopy of trees. Can there be a greater thrill than to glimpse the purple sheen on the wings of the males? Occasionally these descend from the heights around mid-morning to seek minerals such as sodium from evaporating puddles on timber extraction roads. The females are even less frequently seen, spending just a couple of hours from midday actively seeking sallows on which to deposit their eggs.

Butterflies in Woodland

BUTTERFLIES IN WOODLAND

1	White-letter Hairstreak	*Satyrium w-album*
2	Purple Hairstreak	*Quercusia quercus*
3	Speckled Wood	*Pararge aegeria*
4	Gatekeeper	*Pyronia tithonus*
5	White Admiral	*Ladoga camilla*
6	Silver-washed Fritillary	*Argynnis paphia*
7	Purple Emperor	*Apatura iris*
8	Small Pearl-bordered Fritillary	*Boloria selene*

A	Wych Elm	*Ulmus glabra*
B	Oak	*Quercus robur*
C	Cock's-foot	*Dactylis glomerata*
D	Couch Grass	*Elymus repens*
E	Honeysuckle	*Lonicera periclymenum*
F	Sallow	*Salix spp.*
G	Dog Violet	*Viola riviniana*

V.B.

Butterflies in Danger

BY PETER NEWTON-LEWIS

This delightful print illustrates ten distinctly localised butterflies. Very few people in Britain will have seen every one. They are particularly vulnerable as their habitats are so specialised.

The three 'northern' butterflies may well be our oldest 'residents' having established themselves after the last Ice Age. All require spells of warm sunny weather at the flight stage and have a short adult life span. The Scotch Argus, found in sheltered, rough, grassy areas, is locally common up to 500 metres in many areas of Scotland. On sunny August days it is worth inspecting hawkweeds, brambles and heathers for sight of this attractive butterfly. The Mountain Ringlet, in contrast, flies above the 500 metre line. Long-term separation from its continental "cousins" has meant that, with different wing patterns, it is a distinct sub-species. Adults are on the wing from early July when they may be seen feeding on Thyme or Tormentil. The Northern Brown Argus is a member of the family which includes the blues, the *Lycaenidae*. Similar in appearance to the Brown Argus found in southern England it has only one brood, emerging slightly later in the season, and is differentiated by lighter markings on the underwings. Like some other "blues" it is tended by ants during its two middle life cycle stages.

Much further south the Lulworth Skipper, protected as it is by the Lulworth firing ranges, has actually thrived in recent years. Its larval foodplant, Tor Grass, has developed with the decline in sheep and rabbit grazing. It is our smallest and darkest skipper and is distributed in good numbers along the East Dorset coast. The Glanville Fritillary is, like the previous butterfly, on the edge of its European range and found only on the south-western coastal slopes of the Isle of Wight, being on the wing in May and June. The butterfly was once found in several English counties so its location now amply illustrates its vulnerability.

The Silver-studded Blue is shown with its "blue" male and the "brown" female. One can see the problems with identification when the Brown Argus looks superficially similar. This blue is mainly a southern, heathland species and is given its name for the bluish-silver "studs" decorating the underwing edges of both males and females. The key foodplants for the caterpillars are heathers as well as trefoils, Rockrose and Gorse. Numbers of colonies are sadly in rapid decline.

The Small Blue has perhaps the sweetest of Latin names, *Cupido minimus*. It is an exquisite, dainty species that amply fits the description of "vulnerable butterfly". It lives in small colonies in many parts of the British Isles although most frequently in southern, limestone areas. It rarely strays from its home territory, being found first in late May and early June, with a second brood in August. As with some other "blues" it develops a close relationship with ants which serve to protect the larva.

At the top of the picture are the rare and elusive Brown and Black Hairstreaks. They are of the same *Lycaenidae* family as the "blues" and, as shown, are significantly bigger. Both require Blackthorn thickets for their life cycle. They will try the patience of even the most avid butterfly watcher. The Black Hairstreak is only found in sheltered, favoured habitats stretching north-eastwards from Oxford. The number of colonies has, if anything, grown but much of this has been due to the restoration of the coppicing cycle of the Blackthorn. It feeds mainly on aphid honeydew. The Brown Hairstreak is very much a late summer butterfly. Its life cycle is known to involve tending by ants. The habitat is specific in its character with a "master tree" (usually Ash), for the males to bask, feed and display in, located in the basin of its surrounding habitat.

The last species is the wonderful Swallowtail. Found only in the fens of Norfolk we see it feeding on Milk Parsley, the caterpillar foodplant. The biggest of Britain's butterflies, the English Swallowtail is a separate race to those commonly seen in Europe. Its markings are darker, making it, arguably, even more attractive and exciting to watch as it skims over the water and amongst the reed beds.

Butterflies in Danger

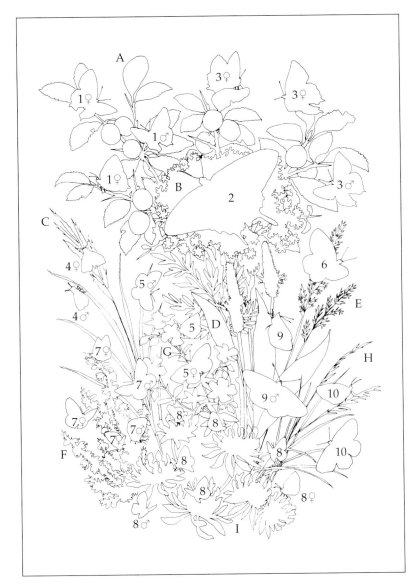

BUTTERFLIES IN DANGER

1	Black Hairstreak	*Satyrium pruni*
2	Swallowtail	*Papilio machaon*
3	Brown Hairstreak	*Thecla betulae*
4	Lulworth Skipper	*Thymelicus acteon*
5	Northern Brown Argus	*Aricia artaxerxes*
6	Scotch Argus	*Erebia aethiops*
7	Silver-studded Blue	*Plebejus argus*
8	Small Blue	*Cupido minimus*
9	Glanville Fritillary	*Melitaea cinxia*
10	Mountain Ringlet	*Erebia epiphron*
A	Blackthorn	*Prunus spinosa*
B	Milk Parsley	*Peucedanum palustre*
C	Tor-grass	*Brachypodium pinnatum*
D	Ribwort Plantain	*Plantago lanceolata*
E	Purple Moor-grass	*Molinia caerulea*
F	Heather	*Calluna vulgaris*
G	Rockrose	*Helianthemum nummularium*
H	Mat-grass	*Nardus stricta*
I	Kidney Vetch	*Anthyllis vulneraria*

Vanishing Butterflies

BY ALAN STUBBS

Whether our scarcest butterflies will vanish from the countryside is up to us. The reason that they are so seldom encountered is all too apparent. Most of the places in which they used to live have changed in character or have been totally destroyed. Their remaining homes are often in great danger, as much through neglect as deliberate destruction.

Chalk grassland is renowned for its richness of colourful butterflies, yet many surviving remnants have lost their special butterflies. The loss of stock grazing, and the decline of rabbits due to myxomatosis as from the 1950s has resulted in grassland becoming rank, even turning to scrub and woodland . To re-create the right conditions needs precise knowledge.

The Silver-spotted Skipper needs short turf on very thin soils where the foodplant, Sheep's Fescue, grows as tussocks with bare soil in proximity. The butterfly darts about but with a quiet approach it is possible to see the silver spots on the underside of the wings.

The Adonis Blue caterpillars need Horseshoe Vetch , where this is 1 - 5cm high. Some bare soil is also useful, even hoof prints, because then the ground gets warmer for caterpillars and adults. The extrovert blue of the male contrasts with the discreet, browner hue of the female.

The Marsh Fritillary lives in wet pastures and on chalk downs with Devil's-bit Scabious, just the sort of places that modern agriculture has drained and ploughed. The sites often need grazing, but, too much or too little and the butterfly may be lost.

The pretty little Duke of Burgundy Fritillary used to be widespread in coppiced woodland where it fed on Primrose. It is humbling that it has been lost from all such sites. Today its caterpillars feed on the strong growth of Cowslips growing snugly at scrub edges. The scrub quickly smothers all sunny intervening gaps so a programme of thinning to maintain glades is essential.

The Wood White has a very casual, floppy flight. It needs a subtle balance of light and shade and the caterpillars feed on such localised plants as yellow Meadow Vetchling and certain other pea plants. Most of its remaining sites are in coniferised plantations as all too often these are the only places where woodland rides have been kept open. If care is not taken, the growing crop of trees soon shades out the rides and paths.

The Pearl-bordered Fritillary used to grace many of our coppiced woods. It thrived on the newly-opened glades where violets provided food for the caterpillars in sunny situations. Most coppiced woods have suffered periods of neglect. Lack of management continuity inevitably led to lack of butterflies. Coppice rotation management is essential where butterflies still remain.

The High Brown Fritillary has been rapidly vanishing. Just in time, some of its woodland sites are being coppiced to save it. However, it is ironic that some of its strongest remaining populations are not in woodland, but in areas of bracken where violets grow - not an obvious conservation priority but a new management challenge.

Another coppice butterfly, the Heath Fritillary, has Cow-wheat as its foodplant. In the early 1980s this butterfly nearly became extinct, such that strong intervention and detailed study were needed. It is a tribute to the work of entomologists, both professional and amateurs, that the Heath Fritillary has been saved from certain extinction.

All the other butterflies in this picture now require similar treatment to survive. Will you let these butterflies vanish ? Or will you join those who are taking action?

Vanishing Butterflies

VANISHING BUTTERFLIES

1	Silver-spotted Skipper	*Hesperia comma*
2	Marsh Fritillary	*Eurodryas aurinia*
3	Heath Fritillary	*Mellicta athalia*
4	Wood White	*Leptidea sinapis*
5	Adonis Blue	*Lysandra bellargus*
6	Duke of Burgundy	*Hamearis lucina*
7	High Brown Fritillary	*Argynnis adippe*
8	Pearl-bordered Fritillary	*Boloria euphrosyne*
A	Sheep's Fescue	*Festuca ovina*
B	Cowslip	*Primula veris*
C	Devil's-bit Scabious	*Succisa pratensis*
D	Cow-wheat	*Melampyrum pratense*
E	Meadow Vetchling	*Lathyrus pratensis*
F	Dog Violet	*Viola riviniana*
G	Horseshoe Vetch	*Hippocrepis comosa*

Migrant Butterflies

BY DR JOHN FELTWELL

The meagre list of some sixty British butterflies would be even shorter if it were not for the migrants which represent about a fifth of the total. We must be thankful for our close proximity to the European mainland. From there our resident populations are topped up, and species such as the Large White and Small White might otherwise be scarce. That might please kitchen gardeners, but not lepidopterists!

First prize for the greatest distance voluntarily travelled by a migrant goes to the Painted Lady, which does a regular haul from North Africa, roughly 1300 kilometres. It's a one-way trip, thus technically 'immigration' for migration is really 'there and back'. In autumn there is a feeble return migration by a few, but it is never completed usually due to bad weather. The Painted Lady is also the world's most cosmopolitan butterfly, thanks to its incredible powers of dispersal.

Clouded Yellows are a delight to see - unmistakable in their rich livery and purposeful flight - always common on the continent, yet always unpredictable migrants to Britain, 1992 being a particularly good year. It is always a challenge to spot a Pale Clouded Yellow amongst fast-moving whites.

The largest migrant on the British list is the Monarch or Milkweed, a presumed involuntary but regular visitor to our shores, since it is really trying in the autumn to fly from the northern parts of North America to south-western states and Mexico. Some of them are thought to get caught up with westerly air streams which blow them westwards and across the Atlantic. Many more undoubtedly perish in the ocean. Monarchs are recorded from the Azores (most westerly outpost of Europe), and now breed on cultivated plants in the Canary Islands, and Spain, offering another source of migrant material.

The Camberwell Beauty has become part of our heritage, since its original encounter during mid-August on Cool Arbour Lane, near Camberwell in 1748. It is not a regular migrant but with good numbers recorded in 1981. Now that processed and packaged timbers are imported as logs to Britain there is less chance that hibernating insects will rise from ships' holds where there used to be a tangle of lichens and other vegetation clinging to old forest trees. However, the thought that some Camberwell Beauties cross the North Sea remains an intriguing possibility.

There is always the chance, when out on a walk in late spring or summer, to come across other migrants. Probably more Long-tailed Blues slip in than are recorded, and Bath Whites are probably overlooked for Small Whites. However, the Queen of Spain Fritillary cannot be confused with anything else, since it has liquid silver on its underside, much befitting its name; its insatiable appetite takes it from flower to flower in a very hurried and powerful manner.

The best places to find migrants are east and south coastal areas (particularly on sea lavender and sea aster) in lucerne or clover fields (oh, that there were more), and colourful gardens with lots of nectar-sources – nectar refuelling stations are essential to thirsty migrants.

So without these colourful masters of the air, Britain's Rhopalocera (butterflies) would be much poorer.

Migrant Butterflies

MIGRANT BUTTERFLIES

1	Painted Lady	*Cynthia cardui*
2	Bath White	*Pontia daplidice*
3	Long-tailed Blue	*Lampides boeticus*
4	Camberwell Beauty	*Nymphalis antiopa*
5	Monarch	*Danaus plexippus*
6	Queen of Spain Fritillary	*Argynnis lathonia*
7	Clouded Yellow	*Colias croceus*
8	Pale Clouded Yellow	*Colias hyale*
A	Sallow	*Salix spp.*
B	Spear Thistle	*Cirsium vulgare*
C	Everlasting Pea	*Lathyrus latifolius*
D	Dog Violet	*Viola riviniana*
E	Red Clover	*Trifolium pratense*

Extinct Butterflies

BY ROBERT GOODDEN

Three of these six British butterflies are very recent extinctions. When population levels become low, extinction can follow with alarming speed. We must look after the wild habitats of butterflies and continue to study their requirements to prevent other species joining the ranks of the extinct.

Having been an abundant species in the 1860s the Black-veined White declined and finally disappeared from Britain in the 1920s. The year 1911 was notable for the species and at times up to this period the larvae were a pest of Kentish orchards. Pesticides are sometimes quoted as the probable cause of the decline, but this may be a convenient hypothesis and the reasons are probably more complex. In the Alps this butterfly is very abundant and congregations of dozens are seen drinking at puddles. The larvae, which feed on Hawthorn, Blackthorn and related fruit trees, are chestnut brown and black, slightly hairy and much more like moth caterpillars.

The fiery, metallic colour of the Large Copper has always captured the imagination of lepidopterists. At one time the East Anglian wetlands were well populated with this butterfly but it became extinct with the draining of the fens in the 1840s. Between the two World Wars, the very similar Dutch race (*L. dispar batavus*) was introduced by Capt. E.B. Purefoy and is still to be found at Woodwalton Fen, but it is closely managed and maintained from captive breeding stock: it always had difficulty in surviving more than a few years without assistance. The larvae feed on Great Water Dock growing at the water's edge.

It has yet to be confirmed whether or not the Large Tortoiseshell is considered extinct in Britain. The butterfly is widely bred in captivity and migratory butterflies almost certainly will appear from time to time. Until the 1950s it was possible to go to known woodlands and find this butterfly regularly breeding, but the decline since then has now reached the stage where there has been no evidence of breeding for a number of years, and not even an authentic sighting for several seasons. The larvae live gregariously, feeding on Elm and Wych Elm, usually in woodland. In Europe the Large Tortoiseshell is still locally common, but noticeably declining.

The Mazarine Blue must be considered as a historic British resident. It was locally abundant in central southern counties, particularly Dorset, in the 1830s but then declined to become an extreme rarity by 1870. There is a record of just one specimen caught in 1902. The Mazarine Blue is a butterfly of meadows and wild grassland. The larvae feed on clovers and allied plants. In Europe the butterfly is very abundant, particularly in mountain regions where grassland has a rich diversity of meadow flowers.

The extinction of the Chequered Skipper around 1975 is, fortunately, only partial, for it has disappeared from England but retains a stronghold in Western Scotland. This spring butterfly lives on grasses in woodland rides and edges but, because of this, it is vulnerable as the woodland grows up and overshadows its breeding areas. There are plans for Butterfly Conservation to re-establish the Chequered Skipper in some of its former localities in the Midlands.

There is no doubt that the life-history of the Large Blue is the most unusual and appealing of any British Butterfly. The caterpillar, having started its feeding life on thyme flowers, finds itself carried off by a red ant and settled underground amongst the brood in its nest. Here the caterpillar spends the winter feeding on the ant larvae, completes its metamorphosis, even emerging from its chrysalis underground, and makes its way through one of the ant tunnels to dry its wings. This was discovered in 1915 by Capt. Purefoy, and subsequently it was found that other species across the world, in the same family (*Lycaenidae*) have a similar way of life. The British Large Blue was declared extinct in 1979. Since then attempts have been successful in re-establishing the species from a Swedish colony and it may once again be seen flying in a number of south-western localities.

Extinct Butterflies

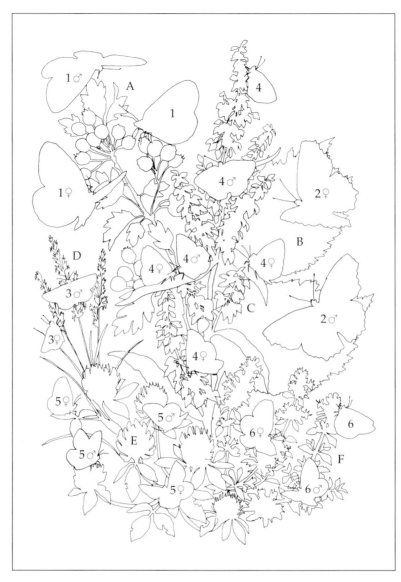

EXTINCT BUTTERFLIES

1	Black-veined White	*Aporia crataegi*
2	Large Tortoiseshell	*Nymphalis polychloros*
3	Chequered Skipper	*Carterocephalus palaemon*
4	Large Copper	*Lycaena dispar*
5	Mazarine Blue	*Cyaniris semiargus*
6	Large Blue	*Maculinea arion*
A	Hawthorn	*Crataegus monogyna*
B	Wych Elm	*Ulmus glabra*
C	Great Water Dock	*Rumex hydrolapathum*
D	Purple Moor-grass	*Molinia caerulea*
E	Red Clover	*Trifolium pratense*
F	Wild Thyme	*Thymus serpyllum*

BUTTERFLY CONSERVATION

BY ANDREW PHILLIPS

Butterfly Conservation is the largest insect conservation society in the world, dedicated to saving wild butterflies and moths and their habitats. It is active on many fronts and priorities are:
- acquisition of reserves
- conservation work and re-establishment of butterfly colonies
- scientific research
- information, education and publicity
- representation, campaigning and lobbying
- fund-raising and sponsorship

None of this comes easily. The conservation of insects, a crucial link in the ecological chain, is an under-developed area of science. Restoring lost butterflies is a complex, resource-intensive task, fraught with practical difficulties.

Extinction, as they say, is forever. England has lost five of its indigenous breeding butterfly species in the past century and a half - that is, one in ten. In the cases of the Large Copper and Large Blue, these were distinct British sub-species, which the world will never see again. As well as these disappearances, there has also been a catastrophic reduction in butterfly numbers overall. It is estimated that for every butterfly alive today in peak season, there may have been one hundred or more a century ago.

What does this tell us about the way we are treating our environment? The decline in butterfly populations has been demonstrating for a long time what is now being shown by reductions in other animal and bird numbers, and confirmed by scientists: that we are exploiting our land, air and water excessively - developing, abusing, despoiling and poisoning without heed for the future.

What can anyone do about this? - All that can be done is to increase awareness of what is happening, try to stop this continuing destruction and attempt to bring back what has been lost. And that is what Butterfly Conservation as an organisation is committed to doing. What is good for butterflies is good for everything else - including man.

To succeed in our aims we need your support. - As a non-profit making charitable organisation most of our work is carried out by members on a voluntary basis. By joining Butterfly Conservation members may also belong to one or more of our local Branches, covering the area in which they live or have an interest. Thereafter, they can attend field trips and lectures, participate in surveys and conservation work parties, fund-raise and join in , even initiate activities which will benefit butterflies and moths.

Butterfly Conservation News, published three time a year, features highlights and achievements of the year. It contains a mixture of news, information and articles designed to interest everyone, expert or lay person, including pieces on gardening, butterflying abroad, new research, ancient history, reserves, Branch events and conservation issues.

The Society also publishes a range of specialist books, including Gardening for Butterflies, Managing Land for Butterflies and Saving Butterflies, a practical guide to the conservation of butterflies in Britain.

For the young today, no longer is it a simple matter of going for a country walk in summertime, and seeing lots of beautiful insects. Butterflies are now, for the most part, difficult to find, unless you know where to look. Our hope is that by the time our youngest members have grown up the situation will have improved, and that they will feel some satisfaction in having contributed to that achievement.

If you are not already a member, please join now and help to save the future.

For further information contact, The Membership Department, Butterfly Conservation, PO Box 222, Dedham, Essex CO7 6EY or telephone (0206) 322342